Elephants

Teaching Tips

Green Level 5

This book focuses on the phonemes /wh/ph/.

Before Reading
- Discuss the title. Ask readers what they think the book will be about. Have them briefly explain why.
- Ask readers to sort the words on page 3. Read the sounds and words together.

Read the Book
- Encourage readers to break down unfamiliar words into units of sound. Then, ask them to string the sounds together to create the words.
- Urge readers to point out when the focused phonics phonemes appear in the text.

After Reading
- Encourage children to reread the book independently or with a friend.
- Ask readers to name other words with /wh/ or /ph/ phonemes. On a separate sheet of paper, have them write the words out.

© 2024 Booklife Publishing
This edition is published by arrangement with Booklife Publishing.

North American adaptations © 2024 Jump!
5357 Penn Avenue South
Minneapolis, MN 55419
www.jumplibrary.com

Decodables by Jump! are published by Jump! Library.
All rights reserved. No part of this book may be reproduced in any form without written permission from the publisher.

Library of Congress Cataloging-in-Publication Data is available at www.loc.gov or upon request from the publisher.

ISBN: 979-8-88996-837-5 (hardcover)
ISBN: 979-8-88996-838-2 (paperback)
ISBN: 979-8-88996-839-9 (ebook)

Photo Credits
Images are courtesy of Shutterstock.com. With thanks to Getty Images, Thinkstock Photo and iStockphoto. Cover – Kletr. 4–5 – Jane Rix, Stu Porter. 6–7 – Maria T Hoffman, Stu Porter. 8–9 – Darwin Brandis, Emma Weil. 10–11 – Avigator Fortuner, Scott Ward. 12–13 – Villiers Steyn, Waridsara_HappyChildren, Alta Oosthuizen. 14–15 – John Michael Vosloo, tanoochai. 16 – Shutterstock.

Can you sort all the words on this page into two groups?

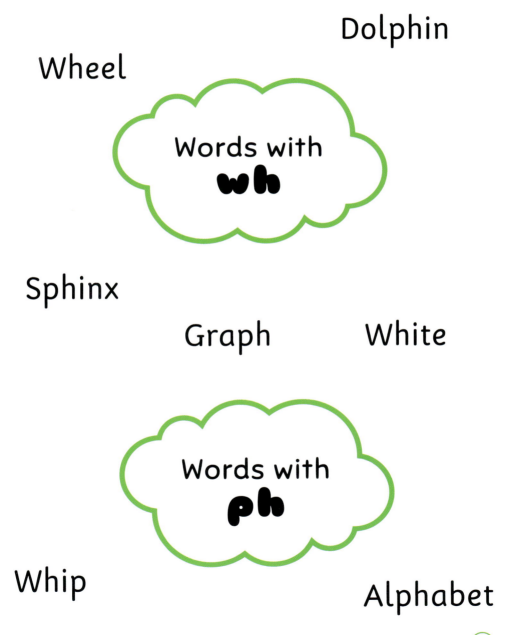

An elephant is a big animal. It has thick skin and a long trunk, which it can swing.

Trunk

Some might have tusks to the right and left of their trunk. Tusks can be up to six feet long!

Tusk

An elephant can whip its trunk back and forth. It can grab food, such as leaves, with its trunk.

An elephant can sniff the air with its trunk. It can smell a drink from far away with just a whiff.

When it is hot, an elephant might cool off with a swim. It can lift its trunk to get air.

An elephant will often suck up and spray mud with its trunk. The mud will stop it from getting sunburnt.

An elephant might harrumph when it is glad. This is when it lets air out of its trunk.

An elephant might express that it is glad with a trunk hug.

A little elephant might suck on its trunk to calm itself, just like a toddler sucks its thumb.

A little elephant is not sure on its feet.
You might see one trip a lot.

A herd will look out for each elephant kid and keep them from harm. They might help an orphan elephant too.

Elephants are big, sweet, and smart. Ralph can paint!

Sound out each word. Does it have a /wh/ or /ph/ sound?

whale   trophy

whiskers   photo